-ag as in flag

Mary Elizabeth Salzmann

Consulting Editor Monica Marx, M.A./Reading Specialist

ABDO
Publishing Company

Published by SandCastle™, an imprint of ABDO Publishing Company, 4940 Viking Drive, Edina, Minnesota 55435.

Printed in the United States.

Credits
Edited by: Pam Price
Curriculum Coordinator: Nancy Tuminelly
Cover and Interior Design and Production: Mighty Media
Photo Credits: Brand X Pictures, Comstock, Corbis Images, Digital Vision, Eyewire Images, Hemera, PhotoDisc

Library of Congress Cataloging-in-Publication Data

Salzmann, Mary Elizabeth, 1968-
       -Ag as in flag / Mary Elizabeth Salzmann.
       p. cm. -- (Word families. Set I)
       Summary: Introduces, in brief text and illustrations, the use of the letter combination "ag" in such words as "flag," "tag," "rag," and "stag."
       ISBN 1-59197-225-6
       1. Readers (Primary) [1. Vocabulary. 2. Reading.] I. Title.

PE1119 .S2342136 2003
428.1--dc21   2002038625

SandCastle™ books are created by a professional team of educators, reading specialists, and content developers around five essential components that include phonemic awareness, phonics, vocabulary, text comprehension, and fluency. All books are written, reviewed, and leveled for guided reading, early intervention reading, and Accelerated Reader® programs and designed for use in shared, guided, and independent reading and writing activities to support a balanced approach to literacy instruction.

Let Us Know

After reading the book, SandCastle would like you to tell us your stories about reading. What is your favorite page? Was there something hard that you needed help with? Share the ups and downs of learning to read. We want to hear from you! To get posted on the ABDO Publishing Company Web site, send us e-mail at:

sandcastle@abdopub.com

SandCastle Level: Transitional

-ag Words

bag

crag

flag

rag

stag

tag

Matt took the fruit out
of the bag.

Kelly and Cal climbed the crag.

Steve waves an
American flag.

Beth washes the car
with a rag.

The stag rests in a field.

Dizzy has a red collar
with a blue tag.

Mag, the Nag, and the Stag

There once was a girl
named Mag.

Mag dreamed that she rode on a nag.

The nag carried her
to the top of a crag.

Mag planted a flag
on the crag.

Then she wiped the crag with a rag.

On the way back,
they met a stag.

Mag, the nag,
and the stag played
a fun game of tag.

The nag and
the stag ran with
a zig and
a zag.

Mag got tired and
began to lag.

She sank to the ground
with a sag.

Then Mag woke up
in her sleeping bag!

The -ag Word Family

bag	nag
crag	rag
drag	sag
flag	snag
gag	stag
jag	tag
lag	wag
Mag	zag

Glossary

Some of the words in this list may have more than one meaning. The meaning listed here reflects the way the word is used in the book.

collar	a thin band of material worn around an animal's neck
crag	a steep rock or cliff
field	a large grassy area
lag	to slow down or fall behind
nag	an old horse
sleeping bag	a padded bag you can sleep in and that zips closed
stag	a male deer

About SandCastle™

A professional team of educators, reading specialists, and content developers created the SandCastle™ series to support young readers as they develop reading skills and strategies and increase their general knowledge. The SandCastle™ series has four levels that correspond to early literacy development in young children. The levels are provided to help teachers and parents select the appropriate books for young readers.

Emerging Readers
(no flags)

Beginning Readers
(1 flag)

Transitional Readers
(2 flags)

Fluent Readers
(3 flags)

These levels are meant only as a guide. All levels are subject to change.

To see a complete list of SandCastle™ books and other nonfiction titles from ABDO Publishing Company, visit www.abdopub.com or contact us at:

4940 Viking Drive, Edina, Minnesota 55435 • 1-800-800-1312 • fax: 1-952-831-1632